# THE COMPLETE FISH COOKBOOK

## Top 100 Modern Favorite Seafood Recipes to Make at Home

### RILEY FLORES

**© COPYRIGHT 2022 ALL RIGHTS RESERVED**

This document is geared towards providing exact and reliable information concerning the topic and issue covered. The publication is sold with the idea that the publisher is not required to render accounting, officially permitted or otherwise qualified services. If advice is necessary, legal or professional, a practiced individual in the profession should be ordered.

In no way is it legal to reproduce, duplicate, or transmit any part of this document in either electronic means or printed format. Recording this publication is strictly prohibited, and any storage of this document is not allowed unless with written permission from the publisher. All rights reserved.

**Warning Disclaimer,** the information in this book is true and complete to the best of our knowledge. All recommendation is made without guarantee on the part of the author or story publishing. The author and publisher disclaim and liability in connection with the use of this information

## Sommario
**INTRODUCTION** ............................................................. 13
**SEAFOOD RECIPES** ....................................................... 14
1. Fast fish soup with vegetables ................................. 14
   ingredients ................................................................ 14
   Preparation steps ..................................................... 15
2. Cold cucumber soup with crayfish ........................... 16
   Ingredients ................................................................ 16
3. Clear fish soup with diced vegetables ...................... 18
   ingredients ................................................................ 18
   preparation ............................................................... 19
4. Shrimp Ginger Soup ................................................. 20
5. Garlic prawns ........................................................... 21
   Ingredients ................................................................ 21
6. Shrimps with garlic .................................................. 22
   ingredients ................................................................ 22
7. Truffle egg dish ........................................................ 24
   ingredients ................................................................ 24
8. Scallops on a skewer ............................................... 25
   ingredients ................................................................ 25
   ☐ salt preparation .................................................... 25
9. Pickled salmon trout sandwich ................................ 27
   ingredients ................................................................ 27
10. Cottage fish spread ................................................ 28
    ingredients ............................................................... 28
11. Fried wild salmon fillet .......................................... 29

ingredients ............................................................. 29
12. Salmon spread with curd cheese ........................ 30
    ingredients ......................................................... 30
13. Smoked trout spread ........................................... 31
    ingredients ......................................................... 31
    ☐ salt preparation ............................................. 31
14. Tuna salad with beans ......................................... 33
    Ingredients ......................................................... 33
15. Pizza toast ............................................................ 34
    ingredients ......................................................... 34
    ☐ toast preparation ........................................... 34
16. Breakfast with salmon trout and egg dish ........ 36
    ingredients ......................................................... 36
17. Cucumber noodles with char sauce .................. 37
    ingredients ......................................................... 37
18. Salmon pancakes rolls ......................................... 38
    ingredients ......................................................... 38
19. The Caribbean flavoured salmon ...................... 39
    ingredients ......................................................... 39
20. Tuna and Cheese Salad ...................................... 40
    ingredients ......................................................... 40
    ☐ pepper preparation ....................................... 40
21. Andalusian prawns .............................................. 42
    ingredients ......................................................... 42
22. Scrambled eggs with truffles ............................. 44
    Ingredients ......................................................... 44

Preparation .................................................. 44
23. Cold cucumber soup with crayfish ................. 45
   ingredients ................................................ 45
24. Truffle egg dish ........................................ 46
   ingredients ................................................ 46
25. Shrimps with garlic .................................... 47
   ingredients ................................................ 47
26. Crayfish in the brew ................................. 48
   ingredients ................................................ 48
27. Organic prawns on wok vegetables ............... 49
   ingredients ................................................ 49
28. Scallops on a skewer ................................ 51
   ingredients ................................................ 51
   ☐ salt preparation ...................................... 51
29. Ceviche made from organic shrimp and avocado .... 52
   ingredients ................................................ 52
   ☐ salt preparation ...................................... 52
30. Shrimp sushi ............................................ 54
   ingredients ................................................ 54
   preparation ............................................... 54
31. Fried scampi ............................................ 55
   ingredients ................................................ 55
32. Calamari with potatoes ............................. 57
   ingredients ................................................ 57
   ☐ parsley preparation .................................. 57
33. Fish in tomato sauce ................................ 58

Ingredients..................................................................58
Preparation.................................................................59
34. Tuna with a fruity cucumber salad........................60
ingredients................................................................60
Preparation steps.....................................................60
35. Fast fish burger......................................................62
ingredients................................................................62
36. Cottage fish spread................................................64
ingredients................................................................64
37. Mayonnaise with basil............................................65
ingredients................................................................65
38. Mayonnaise with basil............................................66
ingredients................................................................66
39. Organic prawns on wok vegetables.......................67
ingredients................................................................67
40. Fried scampi...........................................................69
ingredients................................................................69
41. Pasta with salmon..................................................71
ingredients................................................................71
42. Smoked trout toast................................................72
ingredients................................................................72
43. Smoked Salmon Tartare........................................74
ingredients................................................................74
44. Dutch herring salad................................................75
ingredients................................................................75
☐ chives preparation.................................................75

45. Wrong salmon spread ............................................. 76
    ingredients ............................................................ 76
46. Organic prawns on wok vegetables ................. 77
    Ingredients ............................................................ 77
    preparation ........................................................... 78
47. Tuna noodles .......................................................... 79
    ingredients ............................................................ 79
48. tuna spread ............................................................ 81
    ingredients ............................................................ 81
49. Philadelphia lemon dumplings ........................... 82
    ingredients ............................................................ 82
50. Fast fish burger ................................................... 83
    ingredients ............................................................ 83
51. Fish meatball ......................................................... 85
52. Salmon with sesame crust and broccoli ........ 86
    ingredients ............................................................ 86
    Preparation steps ................................................ 87
53. Salmon and Spinach Pasta .................................. 88
    ingredients ............................................................ 88
    Preparation steps ................................................ 89
54. Coconut curry with salmon and sweet ........... 90
    ingredients ............................................................ 90
    Preparation steps ................................................ 91
55. Skewers of fish and zucchini ............................ 92
    ingredients ............................................................ 92
    Preparation steps ................................................ 92

56. Crostini with crayfish salad .................................. 93
   ingredients .................................................................. 94
   Preparation steps ..................................................... 94
57. fish sticks ................................................................ 96
   ingredients .................................................................. 96
   Preparation steps ..................................................... 96
58. Light And Easy Salmon ..................................... 97
   INGREDIENTS ......................................................... 98
   PREPARATION ....................................................... 98
59. Cuttlefish Salad In Sweet And Sour Sauce ........... 99
   INGREDIENTS ......................................................... 99
   PREPARATION ....................................................... 99
60. Coronello Carpaccio And Dried Cherry Tomatoes ........................................................................ 101
   PREPARATION ..................................................... 102
61. Flag Fish Roll With Smoked Provola ............... 102
   INGREDIENT ......................................................... 103
   PREPARATION ..................................................... 103
62. Vermicelli with Cuttlefish Ink ............................. 104
   INGREDIENT ......................................................... 104
   PREPARATION ..................................................... 104
63. Baked salmon with dill aioli ................................ 105
   Ingredient ................................................................ 106
   Preparation ............................................................. 106
64. Steamed fish fillet on bed of vegetables ............. 107
   ingredients ................................................................ 107

Preparation steps ......................................................... 108
65. Fish and vegetable skewers ............................... 110
   ingredients ............................................................ 110
   Preparation steps .................................................. 110
66. Marinated clams with pepper and parsley ........ 112
   ingredients ............................................................ 112
   Preparation steps .................................................. 112
67. Asparagus and tomato salad .............................. 114
   ingredients ............................................................ 114
   Preparation steps .................................................. 114
68. Fast fish soup with vegetables .......................... 116
   ingre dient s ........................................................... 116
69. Fish in tomato sauce ......................................... 118
   Ingredients ............................................................ 118
   Preparation ........................................................... 119
70. Tuna with a fruity cucumber salad .................... 120
   ingredients ............................................................ 120
   Preparation steps .................................................. 120
71. Fast fish burger ................................................. 122
   ingredients ............................................................ 122
72. Cottage fish spread ........................................... 124
   ingredients ............................................................ 124
73. Cold cucumber soup with crayfish .................... 125
   Ingredients ............................................................ 125
74. Clear fish soup with diced vegetables .............. 127
   ingredi ents ............................................................ 127

75. Grilled anchovies ..................................................... 129
   ingredients ............................................................ 129
76. Fish sausage .......................................................... 131
   ingre dients .......................................................... 131
77. Fish on a stick ....................................................... 133
   ingredients ............................................................ 133
78. Tuna with honey and soy sauce ........................ 134
   ingredients ............................................................ 135
79. Grilled salmon ....................................................... 136
   ingredients ............................................................ 136
80. Peach and fish curry from the steamer .......... 138
   ingredients ............................................................ 138
   preparation .......................................................... 139
81. Fish cabbage roulade ......................................... 140
   ingredients ............................................................ 140
82. Salmon trout pie from the steamer ................ 142
   ingredients ............................................................ 142
83. Fish patties with garden herbs ........................ 144
   ingredients ............................................................ 144
   preparation .......................................................... 145
84. Greek fish soup (Kakavia) .................................. 146
   ingredients ............................................................ 146
85. Salmon with Fennel and Orange from the Air Fryer ........................................................................... 148
   Ingredients ............................................................ 148
86. Lemon Crust Salmon ........................................... 150

ingredients ............................................................. 150
87. Orange salmon with nut rice ................................ 152
   ingredients ............................................................. 152
   Preparation steps ................................................. 152
88. Cured Salmon with Betabel .................................. 154
   Ingredients ............................................................. 154
   ingredients ............................................................. 156
   Preparation steps ................................................. 156
90. Stuffed salmon roll from the grill ........................ 158
   ingredients ............................................................. 158
91. Tuna on a stick ..................................................... 160
   ingredients ............................................................. 160
92. grilled sardines .................................................... 161
   ingredients ............................................................. 162
93. Grilled Sea bream ................................................ 163
   ingredients ............................................................. 163
94. Grilled prawns ...................................................... 165
   ingredients ............................................................. 165
95. Grilled scampi on wok vegetables ....................... 167
   ingredients ............................................................. 167
96. Grilled seafood skewers ...................................... 169
   Preparation steps ................................................. 170
97. Fish skewer with tarator sauce ........................... 171
   ingredients ............................................................. 171
98. Grilled alpine salmon .......................................... 172
   ingredients ............................................................. 173

99. Mediterranean feta in foil ...... 173
    ingredients ...... 174
    preparation ...... 174
100. Ling fish in the foil ...... 175
    ingredients ...... 175
    Preparation steps ...... 175
**CONCLUSION** ...... 177

# INTRODUCTION

If you've never cooked fish or seafood before, you're in for a real treat. The wonderful thing about fish and seafood is that they are frequently prepared in the most basic of ways. This makes an excellent quick meal, and you'll find yourself eating it more frequently than you anticipated.

# SEAFOOD RECIPES

## 1. Fast fish soup with vegetables

**ingredients**

- ½ red pepper
- 50 g small carrots (1 small carrot)
- 1 shallot
- 1 tsp rapeseed oil
- salt
- pepper
- 300 ml fish stock (glass)
- 100 g haddock fillet
- Worcester sauce to taste
- 1 stem flat leaf parsley

**Preparation steps**

1. Core, wash and cut the half bell pepper into thin strips.
2. Wash, clean, peel the carrot, halve lengthways and cut into thin slices. Peel the shallot and dice very finely.
3. Heat oil in a pot. Sauté the paprika, carrot and shallot in it over a medium heat while stirring for 1 minute. Salt and pepper lightly.
4. Pour in the fish stock, bring to the boil, cover and cook gently for 5 minutes.
5. In the meantime, rinse the fish fillet with cold water, pat dry with kitchen paper and cut into bite-sized pieces. Add to the soup and let it simmer for about 5 minutes.
6. In the meantime, wash the parsley, shake dry and pluck the leaves off.
7. Season the soup with Worcestershire sauce, salt and pepper. Stir in the parsley leaves to serve.

## 2. Cold cucumber soup with crayfish

**Ingredients**

- 2 cucumbers (medium)
- 500 ml sour cream (yogurt or buttermilk)
- salt
- Pepper (white, from the mill)
- Dill
- some garlic *For the deposit:*
- 12 crayfish tails (up to 16, freely, raised)
- Cucumber cubes
- Tomato cubes
- Sprigs of dill **preparation**

1. For the cold cucumber soup with crayfish, cook the crabs and release the tails. Peel and core the cucumber and mix with sour cream (yoghurt or buttermilk). Season with salt, pepper, dill and a little garlic. Arrange in pre-chilled plates, place cucumber and tomato cubes, and crab tails and garnish with dill.

## 3. Clear fish soup with diced vegetables

**ingredients**
- 1 l fish stock (clear, strong)
- 250 g pieces of fish fillet (up to 300 g, mixed, without bones, trout, etc.)
- 250 g vegetables (cooked, cauliflower, leek, carrots, etc.)
- salt
- some pepper
- saffron
- some wormwood (possibly dry)
- 1 sprig (s) of dill
- Chervil (or basil, to decorate)

**preparation**

1. Season the finished fish stock with salt, pepper and saffron soaked in a little water and season with a dash of wormwood. Cut the pre-cooked vegetables into small cubes and simmer with the fish fillet for about 4-5 minutes. Arrange quickly in hot plates and garnish with the fresh herbs.

## 4. Shrimp Ginger Soup

**Ingredients:**

- tablespoon full of brown sugar
- 500.0 grams of raw Shrimp
- 20.0 grams of Ginger
- unit of Pepper girl finger
- tablespoon of fish sauce **preparation**

1. Peel the shrimp and remove the entrails.
2. Reserve the heads and shells, wash them well and place them in a pan with water and a pinch of salt.
3. Boil until the broth is reddish (10 minutes), strain and press to extract all the broth.

4. Boil the broth obtained and season with nampla (fish sauce) and brown sugar.
5. Cut the chili pepper and lemon grass, add to the broth together with the kafir lemon leaves and the ginger slices.
6. Add the prawns and boil until they change color.
7. Put the lemon juice in the bowls, pour the hot broth, sprinkle with the chopped cilantro and serve.

## 5. Garlic prawns

**Ingredients**
- 24 prawns (medium-sized, detached and ready to cook)
- 250 ml of olive oil
- 6 pieces of garlic cloves
- 2 pieces of chilli peppers (dried)
- Salt (from the mill) **preparation**

1. Cut the garlic into thin slices, halve the chili peppers, remove the seeds and chop them into small pieces.
2. Heat the olive oil in a pan and fry the garlic and chilli peppers in the hot oil until the garlic takes on a light color.
3. Salt the prawns and fry for about 3 minutes until they are nice and pink.
4. Serve hot.

## 6. Shrimps with garlic

**ingredients**

- 500 g prawns (small, shrimp)
- 1 chilli pepper (red)
- 5 cloves of garlic
- 2 tbsp parsley (finely chopped)
- 1 bay leaf
- olive oil
- Sea salt (from the mill)

- Pepper (from the mill) **preparation**
1. Loosen the prawns from the shell and remove the intestines. Core the chilli pepper and cut into thin half-rings, the garlic finely. Heat the olive oil in a pan and cook the prawns with chilli, garlic and bay leaf for 2 minutes over relatively high heat, stirring constantly. Before serving, season with salt and pepper and sprinkle with chopped parsley.

## 7. Truffle egg dish

**ingredients**

- 100 g shrimp (peeled and cooked)
- 3 egg yolks ☐ 125 ml milk
- 125 ml whipped cream
- Sea salt (from the mill)
- Pepper (white, from the mill)
- 1 tbsp truffle oil **preparation**

1. Whip the milk, cream, egg yolk and truffle oil in stainless steel dishes, stirring constantly over hot steam, until the egg begins to thicken.
2. Roughly chop the shrimp and stir into the truffle egg.
3. Season the truffle egg dish with freshly ground salt and pepper.

## 8. Scallops on a skewer

**ingredients**
- 16 scallops
- 1/2 red pepper *For the marinade:*
- some lime juice
- some peel of an untreated lime
- 1 pinch of curry powder
- salt

**preparation**
1. For the scallops on a skewer, mix the lime juice and zest, curry powder, salt and pepper with the olive oil to a marinade. Place the scallops in the marinade and let them steep for an hour.
2. In the meantime, remove the skin, stones and stem from the bell pepper and cut into squares.

3. Place the scallops and pepper pieces alternately on the wooden skewers. Place on the hot grill and grill each side for about 6 minutes.

## 9. Pickled salmon trout sandwich

**ingredients**

- Ciabatte (or white bread)
- 2 slices of salmon trout (graved)
- 1 tbsp cream cheese (natural)
- 1 teaspoon honey mustard dill sauce
- Lettuce leaves
- Cucumber slices

**preparation**

1. For the sandwich with pickled salmon trout, cut the ciabatta bread in half, spread the lower half with cream cheese and cover with the lettuce leaves.
2. Place the salmon trout slices on top and brush with the honey and mustard sauce. Finish with cucumber slices and the top half of the bread.

## 10. Cottage fish spread

**ingredients**
- 250 g cottage cheese
- 1/2 bunch of chives
- 1 can (s) of tuna (natural)
- salt
- pepper
- 1 squirt of lemon juice

**preparation**
1. For the cottage fish spread, wash and finely chop the chives. Chop up the tuna. Mix the cottage cheese with the chives, tuna and lemon juice.
2. Season with salt and pepper.

## 11. Fried wild salmon fillet

**ingredients**
- 60 days wild salmon fillet
- 8 dag butter
- salt
- pepper
- Chilli flakes **preparation**
1. For the roasted wild salmon fillet, salt and pepper the wild salmon fillets and sprinkle with a few chilli flakes. Heat the butter in a pan and fry the salmon fillets on both sides.
2. Arrange and serve.

## 12. Salmon spread with curd cheese

**ingredients**
- 250 g curd cheese
- 200 g smoked salmon (finely chopped)
- 1/2 lemon (juice)
- salt
- pepper
- Herbs (as desired)

**preparation**
1. Finely chop the smoked salmon.
2. Mix the curd cheese, smoked salmon, lemon juice, herbs of your choice, salt and pepper together well.
3. Season again to taste and serve.

## 13. Smoked trout spread

**ingredients**
- 1 cup of creme fraiche
- 3 eggs (hard-boiled)
- 2 trout (smoked)
- 3 tbsp herbs (chopped)
- pinch of pepper
- 1/2 cup of sour cream
- 1 squirt of lemon juice
- salt

**preparation**

1. For the smoked trout spread, peel the hardboiled eggs cut them finely and place in a bowl. Chop the trout fillets and add.
2. Mix with creme fraiche and sour cream to make a spreadable fish spread. Finally, season with a splash of lemon juice and the chopped herbs.

3. Season to taste with salt and pepper and leave the smoked trout spread in the refrigerator for about 60 minutes.

## 14. Tuna salad with beans

**Ingredients**

- 2 can (s) of tuna (Mexican)
- 1/2 bell pepper (yellow)
- some iceberg lettuce (cleaned and washed)
- tomato
- tbsp vinegar (preferably white wine vinegar)
- 1 tbsp olive oil
- 1 pinch of sugar
- salt
- Pepper (freshly ground) **preparation**

1. For the tuna salad with beans, chop up the iceberg lettuce, mix with vinegar, salt, pepper, a pinch of sugar and oil. Arrange on plates, place the tuna in the centre, garnish

the edge with thinly sliced paprika, quarter the tomatoes and place on top of the tuna. Sprinkle with pepper all around.

## 15. Pizza toast

**ingredients**
- 1/4 stick (s) salami
- 1 pkg of pizza cheese
- 1 can (s) of tuna
- Pizza seasoning
- 1/2 can (s) of corn

☐ toast

**preparation**
1. Cut the salami into small pieces.
2. Then mix all the ingredients together and season with pizza seasoning.
3. Preheat the oven to approx. 200 ° C.

4. Place toast on the baking sheet and distribute the well-mixed ingredients on the bread.
5. Put it in the oven and when the cheese has melted and the bread are lightly browned, the pizza toasts can be enjoyed!

## 16. Breakfast with salmon trout and egg dish

**ingredients**

- 2 slices of rye bread (or wholemeal toast)
- 2 organic eggs (size M)
- 2 tbsp cream cheese (natural)
- 4 slice (s) of salmon trout (pickled)
- some butter
- salt
- Pepper (freshly ground)
- Sprouts (for garnish)

**preparation**

1. For breakfast with salmon trout and egg dish, toast the bread first. Lightly whisk the eggs and prepare an egg dish in a little foamed butter, season with salt and pepper.
2. Brush the bread with cream cheese, spread the egg dish on top and cover with the pickled salmon trout. The breakfast of

salmon trout and scrambled eggs with sprouts garnish.

## 17. Cucumber noodles with char sauce

**ingredients**

- 100 g yoghurt (possibly soy yoghurt)
- 35 g bell peppers (red)
- 1 clove (s) of garlic
- 130 g brook char (smoked)
- 250 g cucumber
- 1 tbsp dille (chopped) **preparation**

1. For the cucumber noodles with char sauce, cut the peppers into small cubes, finely chop the garlic clove, and cut the brook char into small pieces.
2. Mix the yoghurt with the diced paprika, the garlic and the brook trout and season with salt. Cut the cucumber into a noodle shape

with the spiral cutter, mix with the char sauce and serve sprinkled with the dill.

## 18. Salmon pancakes rolls

**ingredients**

- 2 pancakes
- 150 g smoked salmon
- 150 g cream cheese (natural)
- 1 tbsp horseradish (freshly torn)
- 1 teaspoon lemon juice

**preparation**

1. First, mix the cream cheese with the grated horseradish and lemon juice and spread on the pancakes.
2. Place the smoked salmon on the pancakes coated with cream cheese and roll-up.
3. Cut into pieces approx. 3 cm thick and serve.

## 19. The Caribbean flavoured salmon

**ingredients**

- 400 g salmon
- 2 tbsp jerk seasoning
- 2 tbsp margarine (for frying)

**preparation**

1. For the Caribbean salmon, clean the salmon (remove any remaining scales), wash and dry with kitchen paper.
2. Rub both sides with jerk spice. Heat the fat in a pan and fry the salmon on both sides over medium heat.

## 20. Tuna and Cheese Salad

**ingredients**

- 3 handfuls of lettuce (as desired)
- 150 g of cottage cheese
- 1 can (s) of tuna
- 10 tomatoes (small or cocktail)
- 30 g blue cheese
- olive oil
- Balsamic cream
- salt
- pepper

**preparation**

1. For the tuna and cheese salad, wash and dry the lettuce and tomatoes. Divide the lettuce into bite-sized pieces, halve or quarter the tomatoes (depending on size), cut the blue cheese into bite-sized pieces.

2. Mix all ingredients together or place individually on plates, marinate with olive oil and balsamic cream and season with salt and pepper.

## 21. Andalusian prawns

**ingredients**

- 150-200 g prawns (without shell)
- 2 tomatoes
- 1/2 onion
- 6 pcs. Olives (without seeds)
- 1 tbsp parsley (chopped)
- salt
- pepper
- White wine (for pouring)
- Olive oil (for sweating)

**preparation**

1. For the Andalusian prawns, cut the tomatoes and onions into fine cubes. Sweat both in olive oil, add the olives and chopped parsley and season with salt and pepper.

2. Put in the prawns and let stand for 3 minutes.
3. Rinse with white wine, let it get hot for a moment and serve the Andalusian prawns.

## 22. Scrambled eggs with truffles

**Ingredients**

- 100 g shrimp (peeled and cooked)
- 3 egg yolks
- 125 ml of milk
- 125 ml whipped cream
- Sea salt (from the mill)
- Pepper (white, from the mill)
- 1 tbsp truffle oil

**Preparation**

1. Whisk the milk, cream, egg yolk and truffle oil in a stainless-steel bowl, stirring constantly with hot steam until the egg begins to freeze.
2. Roughly chop the prawns and stir into the truffle.
3. Season the truffle eggshell with freshly ground salt and pepper.

## 23. Cold cucumber soup with crayfish

**ingredients**
- 2 cucumbers (medium)
- 500 ml sour cream (yoghurt or buttermilk)
- salt
- Pepper (white, from the mill)
- Dill
- some garlic
- 12 crayfish tails (up to 16, freely, raised)
- Cucumber cubes
- Tomato cubes
- Sprigs of dill

**preparation**

1. For the cold cucumber soup with crayfish, cook the crabs and release the tails. Peel and core the cucumber and mix with sour cream (yoghurt or buttermilk). Season with salt, pepper, dill and a little garlic. Arrange in chilled plates, place cucumber and tomato

cubes as well as crab tails and garnish with dill.

## 24. Truffle egg dish

**ingredients**

- 100 g shrimp (peeled and cooked)
- 3 egg yolks
- 125 ml of milk
- 125 ml whipped cream
- Sea salt (from the mill)
- Pepper (white, from the mill)
- tbsp truffle oil

**preparation**

1. Whip milk, cream, egg yolk and truffle oil in stainless steel dishes, stirring constantly over hot steam until the egg begins to set.
2. Roughly chop the shrimp and stir into the truffle egg.
3. Season the truffle egg dish with freshly ground salt and pepper.

## 25. Shrimps with garlic

**ingredients**
- 500 g prawns (small, shrimp)
- chilli pepper (red)
- 5 cloves of garlic
- tbsp parsley (finely chopped)
- 1 bay leaf
- olive oil
- Sea salt (from the mill)
- Pepper (from the mill)

**preparation**

1. Remove the prawns from the shell and remove the intestines. Core the chilli pepper and cut the garlic finely into thin half-rings. Heat olive oil in a pan and cook the prawns with chilli, garlic and bay leaf for 2 minutes over relatively high heat, stirring constantly.

Before serving, season with salt and pepper and sprinkle with chopped parsley.

## 26. Crayfish in the brew

**ingredients**

- 3 kg crayfish (freshly caught and live)
- 15 liters of salt water
- onion
- Garden herbs (fresh)
- salt
- pepper
- Bay leaf
- 1 leek (s)
- Caraway (fresh) **preparation**

1. Let the freshly caught crayfish boil in the boiling salted water with vegetables and herbs for about 2 - 4 minutes and let it simmer for the same time. All ingredients

are cooked in the brew and this can also be eaten afterwards to detoxify.

## 27. Organic prawns on wok vegetables

**ingredients**

- 10 pieces Yuu n 'Mee Black Tiger organic shrimp (or hand-selected shrimp)
- 60 g eggplant
- 60 g baby corn
- 40 g cherry tomatoes
- 40 g sugar snap peas
- 40 g Chinese cabbage
- 40 g basil (fresh)
- 20 g oyster sauce
- 10 g chilli (green)
- 2 tbsp soy sauce
- 2 pieces of limes (juice of the limes)
- 20 g onion (green)
- 4 tbsp sunflower oil **preparation**

1. For the organic prawns on wok vegetables, gently heat sunflower oil in the wok, sauté the vegetables in it, season with oyster sauce, chillies, lime juice and soy sauce.
2. Add the prawns and top with the basil and serve quickly.

## 28. Scallops on a skewer

**ingredients**
- 16 scallops
- 1/2 red pepper
- some lime juice
- some peel of an untreated lime
- pinch of curry powder
- salt

**preparation**
1. For the scallops on a skewer, mix the lime juice and zest, curry powder, salt and pepper with the olive oil to a marinade. Place the scallops in the marinade and let them steep for an hour.
2. In the meantime, remove the skin, seeds and stem from the pepper and cut into squares.
3. Place the scallops and pepper pieces alternately on the wooden skewers. Place on

the hot grill and grill each side for about 6 minutes.

## 29. Ceviche made from organic shrimp and avocado

**ingredients**
- 20 Yuu´n Mee organic prawns
- 4 avocados
- 2 limes
- chilli peppers (small)
- 1 shallot
- Coriander (fresh)
- garlic
- salt

**preparation**

1. For the ceviche of organic shrimp and avocado, squeeze the limes. Mix the juice with the chopped chilli pepper, the finely sliced shallot, a little garlic and chopped coriander and season with salt.

2. Marinate the prawns with this marinade for about ½ hour.
3. Peel and core the avocados, cut into wedges and season with salt. Serve with the prawns and drizzle the marinade over the ceviche.

## 30. Shrimp sushi

**ingredients**
- 250 g sushi rice (see link in text)
- 200 g Ama Ebi (prawns for sushi)
- Wasabi

**preparation**
1. For shrimp sushi, first prepare the rice according to the basic recipe.
2. Shape the rice into balls with wet hands. Spread a thin layer of wasabi on one side. Place the shrimp on top. Place the shrimp sushi in the hollow of the hand, press the topping smooth and shape into an oval.

## 31. Fried scampi

**ingredients**

- 8 pcs. scampi ((8/12) fresh with head and shell)
- 2 clove (s) of garlic (peeled on)
- 2 sprig (s) of thyme
- olive oil
- salt
- Pepper (mill) **preparation**
1. For the classic fried scampi, first devein the shrimp. To do this, carefully cut into the back with a sharp knife lengthways to the body.
2. The intestine is black and easy to see. Carefully pull this out. Heat a heavy pan, add olive oil, garlic and thyme.

3. Fry the scampi in hot oil for 6-8 minutes, depending on their size. Season with salt and pepper and serve hot.

## 32. Calamari with potatoes

**ingredients**
- 10 calamari
- 8 potatoes
- clove (s) of garlic
- salt
- oil
- butter
- parsley

**preparation**
1. First peel and quarter the potatoes. Bring water to a boil and let the potatoes cook for 10 minutes.
2. Then toss in a pan with the melted butter and the sprig of rosemary, season with salt and garnish with finely chopped parsley.
3. In another pan, fry the calamari for a few minutes with the grated garlic in the oil.

4. Serve the calamari with the potatoes.

## 33. Fish in tomato sauce

**Ingredients**
- 4 frozen white fish fillets of your choice
- 2 cups cherry tomatoes cut in half
- 2 finely sliced garlic cloves
- 120 ml light chicken broth
- 60 ml of dry white wine (or use more chicken stock)
- 1/2 teaspoon salt
- 1/2 teaspoon black pepper
- 1/4 cup finely chopped fresh basil leaves (to garnish)

**Preparation**
1. Place the tomatoes, garlic, salt, and pepper in a pan over medium heat. Cook for 5 minutes or until tomatoes are soft.
2. Add chicken broth, white wine (if used), frozen fish fillets, and chopped basil. Cover and simmer 20-25 minutes, until the fish is fully cooked.
3. Finally, sprinkle with an additional handful of chopped basil and serve on a bed of rice, couscous or quinoa, if desired.

## 34. Tuna with a fruity cucumber salad

**ingredients**

- 2 tuna fillets approx. 130 g each
- salt
- pepper from the mill
- 2 tsp olive oil
- 200 g cucumber
- 150 g Chinese cabbage
- 4 tbsp lime juice
- 4 tbsp chilli chicken sauce
- 4 tbsp orange juice
- 4 tbsp spring onion rings

**Preparation steps**

1. Salt and pepper the tuna fillets. Olive oil in a coated

2. Heat a pan, fry the fish fillets in it for approx. 2 - 3 minutes on each side. Wash the cucumber with the skin and cut into thin slices or slice.
3. Wash and clean the Chinese cabbage and cut into thin strips.
4. Mix the cucumber, Chinese cabbage, lime juice, chilli chicken sauce, orange juice and spring onion rings and season with salt. Arrange the tuna fillets on the salad and serve.

## 35. Fast fish burger

**ingredients**

- 2 fish patties
- some butter
- 2 slice (s) of cheese
- 2 sheets of Güner lettuce
- 4 tomato slices
- 2 burger buns
- tartare sauce
- Ketchup
- onion rings **preparation**

1. For the quick fish burger, fry the fish patties in the pan - at the end of the roasting time, melt a slice of cheese on each of the fish patties.

2. Spread the burger buns with tartar sauce and arrange the lettuce, tomato slices and onion rings on top.
3. Place a fish loaf (with cheese) on each burger bun (with tartare / lettuce/tomato / onion sauce) and top with ketchup.
4. Finish with the burger bun lid.

## 36. Cottage fish spread

**ingredients**

- 250 g cottage cheese
- 1/2 bunch of chives
- 1 can (s) of tuna (natural)
- salt
- pepper
- 1 squirt of lemon juice

**preparation**

1. For the cottage fish spread, wash and finely chop the chives. Chop up the tuna. Mix the cottage cheese with the chives, tuna and lemon juice.
2. Season with salt and pepper.

## 37. Mayonnaise with basil

**ingredients**
- Mayonnaise (bought ready-made or homemade)
- bunch of basil

**preparation**
1. This super-fast basil mayonnaise is an excellent accompaniment to grilled food, fish & chips or homemade fish fingers.
2. Of course, it only goes that fast if you use ready-made mayonnaise. If you prefer to make your own, here is a recipe for homemade mayonnaise.
3. Wash the basil and then shake it dry.
4. Remove the coarse stems. Puree the basil in a blender.

## 38. Mayonnaise with basil

**ingredients**

- Mayonnaise (bought ready-made or homemade)
- 1 bunch of basil

**preparation**

1. This super-fast basil mayonnaise is an excellent accompaniment to grilled food, fish & chips or homemade fish fingers.
2. Of course, it only goes that fast if you use ready-made mayonnaise. If you prefer to make your own, here is a recipe for homemade mayonnaise.
3. Wash the basil and then shake it dry.
4. Remove the coarse stems. Puree the basil in a blender.

## 39. Organic prawns on wok vegetables

**ingredients**

- 10 pieces Yuu n 'Mee Black Tiger organic shrimp
- 60 g eggplant
- 60 g baby corn
- 40 g cherry tomatoes
- 40 g sugar snap peas
- 40 g Chinese cabbage
- 40 g basil (fresh)
- 20 g oyster sauce
- 10 g chilli (green)
- 2 tbsp soy sauce
- 2 pieces of limes (juice of the limes)
- 20 g onions (green)
- 4 tbsp sunflower oil **preparation**
1. For the organic prawns on wok vegetables, gently heat sunflower oil in the wok, sauté the

vegetables in it, season with oyster sauce, chillies, lime juice and soy sauce.
2. Add the prawns and top with basil and serve quickly.

## 40. Fried scampi

**ingredients**

- 8 pcs. scampi ((8/12) fresh with head and shell)
- 2 cloves of garlic (peeled on)
- 2 sprigs of thyme
- olive oil
- salt
- Pepper (mill) **preparation**
1. For the classic fried scampi, first, devein the prawns. To do this, carefully cut into the back with a sharp knife lengthways to the body.
2. The intestine is black and easy to see. Carefully pull this out. Heat a heavy pan, add olive oil, garlic and thyme.

3. Fry the scampi in hot oil for 6-8 minutes, depending on their size. Season with salt and pepper and serve hot.

## 41. Pasta with salmon

**ingredients**

- 250 g spaghetti
- 250 ml whipped cream
- 250 ml of water
- salt
- Spices
- Dill
- 1 cube of herb
- 150 g fish fillets (smoked salmon)

**preparation**

1. Spread the pasta in a closed bowl, sprinkle with whipped cream and water. Season with salt, a little pepper and finely chopped dill.

## 42. Smoked trout toast

**ingredients**

- onion
- 4 smoked trout fillets
- Vegetable oil
- 1/2 can (s) of mushrooms
- 150 g peas (frozen, thawed)
- 4 eggs
- 4 slice (s) of toast
- salt
- Pepper (from the mill) **preparation**

1. For the smoked trout toast, first peel and finely chop the onion. Cut the smoked trout into small pieces or pull apart.

2. Heat some oil in a pan and sweat the onion in it. Add mushrooms and peas. Season to taste with salt and pepper.
3. Whisk the eggs and pour over them.
4. Toast the toast slices and spread the mushroom-pea-egg mixture on top. Top with the trout.
5. Serve the smoked trout toast.

## 43. Smoked Salmon Tartare

**ingredients**

- 1/4 cucumber
- 200 g smoked salmon
- 1/2 bunch of dill
- 1 teaspoon capers
- 1 tbsp lemon juice
- 1 tbsp olive oil
- Salt pepper **preparation**

1. For the smoked salmon tartar, peel the cucumber, cut in half lengthways and core.
2. Cut the pulp into very fine cubes.
3. Finely chop the smoked salmon, finely chop the dill and capers.

4. Mix the cucumber cubes, salmon, dill and capers, stir in lemon juice and olive oil and season the tartar with salt and pepper.

## 44. Dutch herring salad

**ingredients**
- 400 g herrings
- 400 g Gouda
- 100 g pearl onions
- 3 pieces of pickles
- 250 g sour cream
- 3 tbsp mayonnaise
- salt
- pepper
- sugar
- chives

**preparation**
1. Debone and dry the herring fillets.
2. Cut the Gouda cheese, herring, pickles and eggs into bite-sized pieces and stir in a bowl.

3. Whisk the mayonnaise with the sour cream, sugar, pepper and salt. Finely chop the chives and stir into the sauce. Finally, mix in the herring, pearl onion and cheese.

## 45. Wrong salmon spread

**ingredients**

- 250 g curd cheese (lean)
- 4 teaspoons of milk
- 2 glasses of salmon substitute (80 g each)
- salt
- 100 ml whipped cream

**preparation**

1. Mix the curd cheese, milk and salmon substitute in a bowl with a mixer.
2. Season to taste with salt.
3. Finally, whip the whipped cream until stiff and fold in.

## 46. Organic prawns on wok vegetables

**Ingredients**
- 10 pieces Yuu n 'Mee Black Tiger organic shrimp (or hand-selected shrimp)
- 60 g eggplant
- 60 g baby corn
- 40 g cherry tomatoes
- 40 g sugar snap peas
- 40 g Chinese cabbage
- 40 g basil (fresh)
- 20 g oyster sauce
- 10 g chilli (green)
- 2 tbsp soy sauce
- 2 pieces of limes (juice of the limes)

- 20 g onion (green)
- 4 tbsp sunflower oil

**preparation**
1. For the organic prawns on wok vegetables, gently heat sunflower oil in the wok, sauté the vegetables in it, season with oyster sauce, chillies, lime juice and soy sauce.
2. Add the prawns and top with the basil and serve quickly.

## 47. Tuna noodles

**ingredients**
- 1 can (s) of tuna (natural)
- 7 capers
- 1/2 glass of tomatoes (dried, in oil; alternatively, fresh tomatoes)
- 7 olives
- 1/2 onion
- Chili oil
- garlic oil
- 250 g spaghetti

**preparation**
1. Cut the onion into small cubes. Dice the sundried tomatoes and drain the tuna.
2. Cook the spaghetti according to the instructions on the packet.

3. Put the chilli and garlic oil in a pan and sauté the onion. Add tomatoes, capers, olives and tuna. Let it simmer briefly, add a little pasta water and add lemon juice.
4. Arrange the cooked pasta with the sauce and serve.

## 48. tuna spread

**ingredients**

- 1 can (s) of tuna (in its own juice, drained)
- 130 g sour cream
- 1 tbsp mayonnaise
- 1 tbsp capers
- 1 dash of lemon juice
- salt
- Pepper (from the mill)

**preparation**

1. For the tuna spread, first drain the capers and chop them finely.
2. Mix all ingredients well to form a smooth tuna spread.

## 49. Philadelphia lemon dumplings

**ingredients**

- 175 g Philadelphia double cream setting natural
- 20 g flour (handy)
- 1/2 lemon
- 1 pc egg
- 20 g butter (melted)
- A bit of salt
- 1 tbsp white breadcrumbs (fine) **preparation**

1. For the Philadelphia lemon dumplings, grate the zest of half a lemon and then squeeze half a lemon.
2. Mix all ingredients together and cut out dumplings with a wet tablespoon.
3. Put the dumplings in boiling water and let stand for about 3 minutes.

## 50. Fast fish burger

**ingredients**
- 2 fish patties
- some butter
- 2 slice (s) of cheese
- 2 sheets of Güner lettuce
- 4 tomato slices
- 2 burger buns
- tartare sauce
- Ketchup
- onion rings **preparation**

1. For the quick fish burger, fry the fish patties in the pan - at the end of the roasting time, melt a slice of cheese on each of the fish patties.

2. Spread the burger buns with tartar sauce and arrange the lettuce, tomato slices and onion rings on top.
3. Place a fish loaf (with cheese) on each burger bun (with tartare / lettuce/tomato / onion sauce) and top with ketchup.
4. Finish with the burger bun lid.

## 51. Fish meatball

- cooking time 10mins
- servings 1
- calories 235 **ingredients**
- 100 g tuna (can)
- 1 piece of eggs (60 g)
- 1/2 tbsp wheat flour (whole grain)
- 1 pinch of iodine salt
- 1 pinch of black pepper **preparation**

1. Mince the tuna in a bowl.
2. Add egg white, flour, salt and pepper and mix everything.
3. Shape meatballs and fry until golden brown on each side.

## 52. Salmon with sesame crust and broccoli

**ingredients**
- 600 g broccoli
- iodized salt with fluoride
- 1 clove of garlic
- 15 g ginger
- 480 g very fresh salmon fillet (8 pieces)
- pepper
- 30 g sesame
- 15 g coconut oil (1 tbsp)
- 2 tbsp sesame oil
- chilli thread
- 50 ml vegetable broth
- 2 tbsp lime juice
- 1 lime

**Preparation steps**
1. Wash the broccoli, wash it and cut it into small bunches. Boil in boiling water with salt for 4 minutes, drain, rinse and drain well. In the meantime, peel the garlic and chop it. Peel the ginger and grate it finely. Rinse the salmon with cold water, wipe off the water, season with salt and pepper, and sprinkle with sesame seeds.
2. Heat coconut oil in a pan and bake the salmon skin on medium heat until golden brown. Then turn the other side over until golden brown and fry. Place on an ovencompatible plate or baking sheet and soak in an oven preheated to 100 ° C for approximately 10 minutes (convection is not recommended; gas: minimum setting) (the interior should still be glassy).
3. Meanwhile, heat sesame oil in a pan and fry garlic and ginger. Add broccoli and chili threads, mix, season with soup stock, and season with salt, pepper, and lime juice. Rinse the lime with boiling water, tap it lightly to drain it, and cut it into a comb shape. Divide 2 slices of salmon and broccoli

vegetables into 4 dishes and decorate with lime combs.

## 53. Salmon and Spinach Pasta

**ingredients**

- 500 g whole wheat pasta (e.g. penne)
- salt
- 1 clove of garlic
- 1 red onion
- 1 organic lemon
- 2 tbsp olive oil
- 300 ml vegetable broth
- 3 tbsp cream cheese
- 250 g salmon fillet
- 80 g spinach
- Pepper

**Preparation steps**

1. Cook the pasta in plenty of boiling salted water according to the instructions on the package. Then drain.
2. In the meantime, peel the garlic and onion and cut into fine cubes. Rinse the lemon with hot water, pat dry and rub the peel.
3. Heat the oil in a pan, fry the garlic and onions over medium heat until translucent. Add lemon zest and pour in the vegetable stock. Stir in the cream cheese and bring to the boil once. Then reduce the heat.
4. Cut the salmon fillet into bite-sized pieces, add to the sauce, and cook for about 5 minutes.
5. Wash the spinach and spin dry. Add to the salmon with the noodles, season with pepper and mix well. Spread the salmon pasta with spinach on four plates and serve.

## 54. Coconut curry with salmon and sweet potatoes

**ingredients**
- 150 g whole grain basmati rice
- salt
- 1 onion
- 3 garlic cloves
- 1 red chilli pepper
- 20 g ginger (1 piece)
- 600 g sweet potatoes (2 sweet potatoes)
- 200 g celery (3 sticks)
- 20 g coriander (1 bunch)
- 400 g salmon fillet
- 1 tsp sesame oil
- 1 tsp cumin
- 1 tsp coriander

- ½ tsp turmeric powder
- 150 ml coconut milk (9% fat)
- 300 ml vegetable broth
- 2 tbsp fish sauce

**Preparation steps**

1. Cook rice in 2.5 times the amount of boiling salted water according to the package instructions for about 35 minutes.
2. In the meantime, peel the onion and garlic and cut into small cubes. Halve the chilli lengthways, core, wash and chop. Ginger peel and finely chop. Peel the sweet potatoes and cut into cubes. Clean the celery, remove the threads if necessary, wash and cut into small pieces. Wash the coriander, shake dry and pluck the leaves. Rinse the salmon fillet, pat dry and roughly dice.
3. Heat oil in a pot. Sauté the onion, garlic, ginger and chilli over a medium heat for 2-3 minutes. Add the spices and sauté them. Deglaze with coconut milk and stock and bring to the boil.
4. Add celery and sweet potato cubes and cook on a low heat for 10 minutes. Add salmon and cook for another 4-5 minutes. Season

coconut curry with fish sauce and serve with rice and coriander.

## 55. Skewers of fish and zucchini

**ingredients**

- 300 g salmon fillet ready to cook, skinless
- 300 g cod fillet ready to cook, skinless
- 1 tbsp lemon juice
- 2 zucchinis
- 150 g pineapple
- pepper from the mill
- sea-salt

**Preparation steps**

1. Wash the fish fillets, pluck them dry, cut into bite-sized cubes, and mix them with lemon juice. Wash and clean the zucchini and

quarter lengthways and 2/3 of the zucchini into 1.5 cm wide pieces and cut the rest into narrow slices. Cut the pineapple into bitesized pieces.

2. Stick the zucchini with the fish and optionally the pineapple on wooden skewers. Start with a thick piece of zucchini or a piece of pineapple, then a cube of salmon, then a thin slice of zucchini, a piece of cod and finally another thick piece of zucchini. Grill the skewers on a hot grill until golden brown, turning them occasionally, arrange in a bowl or pan and serve sprinkled with pepper and sea salt.

## 56. Crostini with crayfish salad

**ingredients**

- 12 slices whole grain baguette
- 2 spring onions
- 2 tbsp creme fraiche cheese
- 2 tbsp sour cream
- 1 tsp mustard
- 350 g crayfish meat
- 2 tbsp freshly chopped dill
- lemon juice
- salt
- pepper
- dill tips for garnish

**Preparation steps**

1. Place the bread slices on a rack and toast them in the preheated oven with the grill function on both sides until crispy and golden brown.
2. Take out of the oven and let cool down a bit. Wash and clean the spring onions and cut into rings. Mix with the crème fraîche, sour cream and mustard and mix in the crayfish and dill. Season the crayfish salad with lemon juice, salt and pepper and spread over the slices of bread.

3. Serve the crostini with crayfish salad garnished with dill tips.

## 57. fish sticks

**ingredients**

- 4 fish fillets z. b. pollack, pangasius
- 2 tbsp lemon juice
- salt
- pepper
- 2 tbsp flour for turning
- 2 eggs
- 4 tbsp breadcrumbs
- 1 tbsp cornflakes at will
- 2 tbsp clarified butter for frying

**Preparation steps**

1. Thaw the fish fillets or dab off fresh ones and divide each into three to four even

pieces. Drizzle the fish with lemon juice and let it steep a little.
2. In the meantime, put the flour, eggs and breadcrumbs each in plates. Whisk eggs well with a fork. Crumble the cornflakes as desired and mix with breadcrumbs.
3. Heat clarified butter in a pan.
4. Season the fish pieces with salt and pepper, turn them lightly in the flour, dip them all around in the egg and finish breading them in the crumbs. Bake the fish pieces on all sides for approx. 7 minutes until golden brown and serve hot.

## 58. Light And Easy Salmon

## INGREDIENTS

- .4 salmon steaks.
- 2 tablespoon (s) of mustard.
- 2 tablespoon (s) tablespoon juice of lemon ☐ parsley. ☐ salt.
- pepper

## PREPARATION

1. Preheat your oven to 200 ° C.
2. Arrange your salmon steaks in a non-stick ovenproof dish.
3. In a bowl, combine the mustard and lemon juice.
4. Sprinkle the steaks with this preparation.
5. Salt and pepper (unless you are using a strong mustard!)
6. Chop a little parsley and place it on the fish.
7. Bake your light and easy salmon steaks for 20 minutes in a hot oven.

## 59. Cuttlefish Salad In Sweet And Sour Sauce

**INGREDIENTS**

- 550 g of fresh cuttlefish
- 30 g of raisins
- 20 g of pine nuts
- 80 g of oil
- 60 g of vinegar rose grapes
- Salt to taste
- Parsley in leaves
- 1 head of radicchio

**PREPARATION**

Clean the cuttlefish and blanch in the water, the fins and the weave take longer. Cool and cut into julienne strips.

Clean the radicchio and cut it thinly.

In a steel bowl mix cuttlefish, radicchio, raisins, pine nuts, vinegar, oil, salt and a teaspoon of sugar.

Leave to marinate and flavor. Serve in a radicchio leaf. Decorate with parsley leaves.

## 60. Coronello Carpaccio And Dried Cherry Tomatoes

**INGREDIENTS:**

- Coronello (stockfish fillet) 500gr.
- Dried cherry tomatoes
- Black olives
- Extra virgin olive oil
- White pepper
- Capers "lacrimelle"
- Pomegranate or wild strawberries (depending on the season)

**PREPARATION**
1. The main component of this dish, but like all dishes, in addition to the freshness of any ingredient, consists in the high quality of the stockfish and in the right salting, otherwise you risk upsetting the simplicity of the dish itself.
2. The Coronello is peeled and the dish is mounted as if the gills were so many petals. It is a kind of tapenade of olives and cherry tomatoes and rests harmoniously on the coronello petals, together with the desalted capers.
3. Decorate the whole with pomegranate grains or with the pickled strawberries.

### 61. Flag Fish Roll With Smoked Provola

## INGREDIENT

- 2 kg of fish flag
- 150g smoked cheese
- bread grated
- extra-virgin olive oil
- salt, capers, garlic and parsley
- Fillet the flag fish, making 30 cm fillets each.

## PREPARATION

1. Compose the filling with a smoked provola nut, grated bread, capers and minced garlic, wrap the fillets on themselves, bread them in the breadcrumbs. Bake at a temperature of 180 ° for about 5-7 minutes.
2. Pour a drizzle of extra virgin olive oil over the fillets and decorate with parsley leaves.

## 62. Vermicelli with Cuttlefish Ink

## INGREDIENT

- 320 grams of linguine, vermicelli or spaghetti, even spaghettoni
- 3 very fresh squid ink pockets
- 250 gr. of cuttlefish
- 1 clove of garlic
- A very fresh lemon
- Extra virgin olive oil
- Fresh mint leaves

## PREPARATION

1. Clean the cuttlefish well, peel them and carefully collect the black bags and set them aside. Brown in a large pan 8 tablespoons of extra virgin olive oil with the whole garlic and just crushed, pour the welldried

cuttlefish cut into small pieces and fry for 2 minutes.
2. At the same time cook the vermicelli or spaghetti or even spaghetti in abundant salted water.
3. In a bowl mix the cuttlefish black pasta in very little cooking water and pour it into the pan with the cuttlefish sauce, mixing well.
4. Strain the pasta al dente with a couple of minutes in advance and finish cooking by sautéing it in the pan with the dressing of the cuttlefish and the black, 2 drops of lemon each and, if necessary, add the pasta cooking water.

## 63. Baked salmon with dill aioli

**Ingredient**

- 4 salmon fillets with skin, approximately 170 g each
- tablespoon (7.5 ml) avocado oil Zest of ½ large lemon ☐ Kosher salt
- Freshly ground black pepper

*Alioli To Drop*

- ½ cup (120 ml) of Primal Kitchen mayonnaise or other mayonnaise suitable for the paleolithic diet
- 2 small sliced garlic cloves
- 2 teaspoons (15 ml) freshly squeezed lemon juice
- 1 tablespoon (15 ml) chopped fresh dill
- teaspoon (1 ml) kosher salt
- teaspoon (1 ml) freshly ground black pepper zest of ½ large lemon

**Preparation**

1. This salmon fillet baked at low temperature melts in the mouth. Prepared like this, the salmon is pretty pink, so don't be alarmed when you take it out of the oven and it still looks raw. On the contrary, it will be the best made fish you've ever eaten!

2. Preheat the oven to 135 ° C. Put the salmon fillets in an iron pot or baking dish. Mix the oil with half the lemon zest and paint the top of the fish. Salt and pepper Bake the salmon between sixteen and eighteen minutes, until it can be divided into small pieces with a fork.
3. While the salmon is in the oven, mix the mayonnaise with the garlic, zest and lemon juice, dill, salt and pepper.
4. Serve the salmon accompanied by the aioli.

## 64. Steamed fish fillet on bed of vegetables

**ingredients**

- 1 shallot

- ½ tuber fennel
- 60 g small carrots (1 small carrot)
- 3 tbsp classic vegetable broth
- salt
- pepper
- 70 g pangasius fillet (preferably organic pangasius)
- 2 stems flat leaf parsley
- ½ small lime

**Preparation steps**

1. Peel and finely dice shallot.

Clean and wash the fennel and carrot, peel the carrot thinly. Cut both vegetables into narrow sticks.

3. Heat the broth in a coated pan. Add the shallot, fennel and carrot and cook for about 3 minutes. Season to taste with salt and pepper.
4. Rinse the fish fillet, pat dry, lightly salt and place on the vegetables. Cover and simmer on a low heat for 8-10 minutes.
5. In the meantime, wash the parsley, shake dry, pluck the leaves and finely chop with a large knife.
6. Squeeze half a lime and drizzle the juice over the fish to taste. Pepper to taste, sprinkle with the parsley and serve.

2.

## 65. Fish and vegetable skewers

### ingredients

- 250 g ripe mango (1 small mango)
- 1 lime
- 150 g zucchini (1 small zucchini)
- 4 cherry tomatoes
- 200 g cod fillet
- salt
- ½ tsp yogurt butter
- pepper
- 1 tsp pink pepper berries
- 100 g yogurt (0.1% fat)

### Preparation steps

1. Peel the mango. Cut the pulp from the stone in thick wedges and dice.

Halve the lime and squeeze out the juice.
3. Wash, clean and dice the zucchini. Wash tomatoes.
4. Rinse the cod fillet, pat dry with kitchen paper and cut into cubes of the same size. Salt.
5. Melt the butter in a small pan. Stir in 2 tablespoons of lime juice and a little pepper and remove from heat.
6. Put the fish cubes, mango, tomatoes and zucchini on wooden skewers and brush all around with the lime butter.
7. Cook the skewers in a grill pan over medium heat or on the hot grill for 8-10 minutes. Turn once.
8. In the meantime, lightly mash the pepper berries with the back of a knife and mix with the yogurt in a small bowl. Season with salt and the remaining lime juice, serve with the fish and vegetable skewers.

2.

## 66. Marinated clams with pepper and parsley

**ingredients**
- 1 kg fresh or frozen clams
- 1 large onion
- 2 garlic cloves
- 1 green pepper
- ½ fret flat leaf parsley
- ½ lemon
- 2 tbsp olive oil
- 275 ml dry white wine or fish stock
- salt
- pepper

**Preparation steps**
1. Brush off clams and place in cold water for 1 hour; change the water once. (Thaw frozen mussels.)

In the meantime, peel the onion and garlic and cut into fine cubes. Halve the pepper lengthways, remove the core, wash and cut into fine strips.
3. Wash the parsley, shake dry, pluck the leaves off and roughly chop. Squeeze the lemon.
4. Drain the clams in a colander. Sort out the opened mussels.
5. Heat the oil in a large saucepan and sauté the onion and garlic until translucent. Add the pepper and sauté briefly.
6. Pour in white wine and bring to the boil.
7. Add the clams and cook covered over high heat for about 4 minutes until all the clams have opened, shaking the pot several times.
8. Take the clams out of the pot with a slotted spoon and place on a platter. Sort out any mussels that have not opened.
9. Add the parsley to the stock, season with salt, pepper and lemon juice.
10. Pour the stock over the clams and serve immediately or chilled.

2.

## 67. Asparagus and tomato salad

**ingredients**
- 1 lemon
- 1 red onion
- 1 bunch dill
- 200 g cherry tomatoes
- 150 g deep sea shrimp (ready to cook)
- 2 tbsp olive oil
- 1 tsp agave syrup or honey
- salt black pepper
- 500 g white asparagus

**Preparation steps**
1. Squeeze the lemon. Peel the onion and cut into fine strips. Wash the dill, shake dry and chop. Wash tomatoes and cut in half.

Put lemon juice, onions, dill and tomatoes in a

bowl with prawns, oil and agave syrup. Salt, pepper and mix well.
2. Wash the asparagus and peel it thoroughly with the peeler. Cut off the woody ends and slice the sticks diagonally. Leave the asparagus tips whole.
3. Bring a sufficiently large saucepan of salted water to the boil and cook the asparagus in it for 4-5 minutes until al dente.
4. Drain the asparagus in a sieve and drain well.
5. Add to the other ingredients while still warm and mix thoroughly. Let it steep for 3 minutes, season again with salt and pepper and serve.

## 68. Fast fish soup with vegetables

**ingredients**

- ½ red pepper
- 5 small

carrots (1 small carrot)
- 1 shallot
- 1 tsp rapeseed oil
- salt
- pepper
- 300 ml fish stock (glass)
- 100 g haddock fillet
- worcester sauce to taste
- 1 stem flat leaf parsley

**Preparation steps**

1. Core, wash and cut the half bell pepper into thin strips.
2. Wash, clean, peel the carrot, halve lengthways and cut into thin slices. Peel the shallot and dice very finely.
3. Heat oil in a pot. Sauté the paprika, carrot and shallot in it over a medium heat while stirring for 1 minute. Salt and pepper lightly.
4. Pour in the fish stock, bring to the boil, cover and cook gently for 5 minutes.
5. In the meantime, rinse the fish fillet with cold water, pat dry with kitchen paper and cut into bite-sized pieces. Add to the soup and let it simmer for about 5 minutes.
6. In the meantime, wash the parsley, shake dry and pluck the leaves off.

7. Season the soup with Worcestershire sauce, salt and pepper. Stir in the parsley leaves to serve.

## 69. Fish in tomato sauce

**Ingredients**
- 4 frozen white fish fillets of your choice
- 2 cups cherry tomatoes cut in half
- 2 finely sliced garlic cloves
- 120 ml light chicken broth
- 60 ml of dry white wine (or use more chicken stock)
- 1/2 teaspoon salt
- 1/2 teaspoon black pepper
- 1/4 cup finely chopped fresh basil leaves (to garnish)

**Preparation**
1. Place the tomatoes, garlic, salt, and pepper in a pan over medium heat. Cook for 5 minutes or until tomatoes are soft.
2. Add chicken broth, white wine (if used), frozen fish fillets, and chopped basil. Cover and simmer 20-25 minutes, until the fish is fully cooked.
3. Finally, sprinkle with an additional handful of chopped basil and serve on a bed of rice, couscous or quinoa, if desired.

## 70. Tuna with a fruity cucumber salad

**ingredients**
- 2 tuna fillets approx. 130 g each
- salt
- pepper from the mill
- 2 tsp olive oil
- 200 g cucumber
- 150 g Chinese cabbage
- 4 tbsp lime juice
- 4 tbsp chilli chicken sauce
- 4 tbsp orange juice
- 4 tbsp spring onion rings

**Preparation steps**
1. Salt and pepper the tuna fillets. Olive oil in a coated

2. Heat a pan, fry the fish fillets in it for approx. 2 - 3 minutes on each side. Wash the cucumber with the skin and cut into thin slices or slice.
3. Wash and clean the Chinese cabbage and cut into thin strips.
4. Mix the cucumber, Chinese cabbage, lime juice, chilli chicken sauce, orange juice and spring onion rings and season with salt. Arrange the tuna fillets on the salad and serve.

## 71. Fast fish burger

**ingredients**
- 2 fish patties
- some butter
- 2 slice (s) of cheese
- 2 sheets of Güner lettuce
- 4 tomato slices
- 2 burger buns
- tartare sauce
- Ketchup
- onion rings **preparation**

1. For the quick fish burger, fry the fish patties in the pan - at the end of the roasting time, melt a slice of cheese on each of the fish patties.

2. Spread the burger buns with tartar sauce and arrange the lettuce, tomato slices and onion rings on top.
3. Place a fish loaf (with cheese) on each burger bun (with tartare / lettuce/tomato / onion sauce) and top with ketchup.
4. Finish with the burger bun lid.

## 72. Cottage fish spread

**ingredients**

- 250 g cottage cheese
- 1/2 bunch of chives
- 1 can (s) of tuna (natural)
- salt
- pepper
- 1 squirt of lemon juice

**preparation**

1. For the cottage fish spread, wash and finely chop the chives. Chop up the tuna. Mix the cottage cheese with the chives, tuna and lemon juice.
2. Season with salt and pepper.

## 73. Cold cucumber soup with crayfish

**Ingredients**
- 2 cucumbers (medium)
- 500 ml sour cream (yogurt or buttermilk)
- salt
- Pepper (white, from the mill)
- Dill
- some garlic For the deposit:
- 12 crayfish tails (up to 16, freely, raised)
- Cucumber cubes
- Tomato cubes
- Sprigs of dill **preparation**

2. For the cold cucumber soup with crayfish, cook the crabs and release the tails. Peel and core the cucumber and mix with sour cream (yoghurt or buttermilk). Season with salt,

pepper, dill and a little garlic. Arrange in pre-chilled plates, place cucumber and tomato cubes, and crab tails and garnish with dill.

## 74. Clear fish soup with diced vegetables

**ingredi ents**
- 1 l fish stock (clear, strong)
- 250 g pieces of fish fillet (up to 300 g, mixed, without bones, trout, etc.)
- 250 g vegetables (cooked, cauliflower, leek, carrots, etc.)
- salt
- some pepper
- saffron
- some wormwood (possibly dry)
- 1 sprig (s) of dill
- Chervil (or basil, to decorate) **preparation**
2. Season the finished fish stock with salt, pepper and saffron soaked in a little water and season with a dash of wormwood. Cut the

pre-cooked vegetables into small cubes and simmer together with the fish fillet for about 4-5 minutes. Arrange quickly in hot plates and garnish with the fresh herbs.

## 75. Grilled anchovies

**ingredients**

- 1 kg of anchovies
- some salt (coarse)
- some olive oil
- 1 sprig (s) of rosemary **preparation**

1. For grilled anchovies, first clean the anchovies, remove the gills and cut off the heads.
2. Make a cut on the side along the backbone and dry well with a paper towel. Salt the anchovies only on the outside with coarse salt.
3. Heat up the grill well and oil a little with olive oil. Fry the anchovies on both sides for

3 to 5 minutes. Turn the fish only once. In between, brush with the sprig of rosemary dipped in olive oil.
4. Grill the anchovies until the skin is goldenbrown and crispy.
5. The grilled anchovies serve immediately.

## 76. Fish sausage

**ingredients**

- 500 g wild salmon fillet
- 500 g pollack fillet
- 1 tbsp sea salt
- 1 teaspoon pepper
- 1 squirt of lemon juice
- 1 bunch of dill
- 1 bunch of tarragon
- 1 bunch of parsley
- Sheep intestines (order the required amount of fish meat from the butcher)

**preparation**

1. For the fish sausage, first let the sheep intestine soak in lukewarm water (not over 40 degrees) for about an hour before sausage. This makes the natural casing more elastic and easier to process.)
2. Finely chop the fish fillet with the knife.
3. Finely chop the onions, parsley, tarragon and dill and knead into the fish mixture together with a little lemon juice, sea salt and pepper. (If you want, you can fry some of the fish mass in a pan for testing and add seasoning if necessary.)
4. Then the filler is filled with the fish mass and the sheep intestine is pulled onto the filler neck. The end of the natural casing is knotted.
5. Fill the sheep intestine carefully and not too tightly with the fish mixture and twist it into the desired sausage length.
6. The fish sausages can be cooked on the grill over direct medium heat or on the stove in the pan.

## 77. Fish on a stick

**ingredients**

- 8 whitefish (roach, Näslinge, bream, barbel, etc.)
- salt
- 8 softwood skewers (approx. 50 cm long)
- Charcoal embers (green wood)
- Potatoes (to taste)
- Aluminum foil **preparation**

1. Fish on a stick are easy to prepare on the garden grill.
2. The fish are first gutted, cleaned well, scaled if necessary, washed and patted dry with kitchen paper. Then you cup them with a very sharp knife by cutting them on both sides at intervals of approx. 2 mm.

3. The fish are salted well inside and out, whereby the salt should act for about 1/2 to 1 hour. Then stick them on the wooden skewers.
4. Then the fish are slowly fried over the charcoal embers enriched with green wood until they are crispy and crispy. The green wood, which forms a lot of smoke, is needed because the fish on a stick should be both grilled and smoked.
5. Fry potatoes wrapped in aluminum foil and serve well salted with the fish on the sticks.

## 78. Tuna with honey and soy sauce

**ingredients**

- 4 pieces of tuna steaks
- 2 spring onions (chopped)
- 10 cm ginger
- 125 ml soy sauce
- 2 tbsp honey
- 2 tbsp balsamic vinegar

**preparation**

1. For the marinade, mix the soy sauce with the balsamic vinegar and honey.
2. Put the tuna with the ginger and spring onions in a dish. Pour the marinade on top and put everything in the fridge for 1 hour.
3. After the soaking time, grill the tuna on the grill or in the pan for 3 to 4 minutes on each side.

## 79. Grilled salmon

**ingredients**

- 200 g orange fillets (or orange slices)
- 2 spring onions
- 250 g salmon fillet ( skinless, fresh or frozen and thawed)
- salt
- pepper
- 6 tbsp KUNER Caribbean sauce **preparation**

1. For the grilled salmon, first cut orange fillets or slices into pieces. Clean the spring onions and cut into rings. Cut the salmon into bite-sized pieces, season with salt and

pepper to taste. Carefully mix the Caribbean sauce with the fish, oranges and onions.
2. For each parcel, spread out the aluminum foil twice, approx. 20 x 20 cm. Pour a quarter of the mixture on top and fold and seal the aluminum foil over the filling. Cook the parcels on the hot grill for about 20 minutes.
3. Serve the salmon from the grill.

## 80. Peach and fish curry from the steamer

**ingredients**

- 400 g catfish
- 3 tbsp soy sauce
- 1 tbsp lime juice
- salt
- pepper
- some ginger
- 1 clove (s) of garlic
- 1 pc. Chili peppers
- 2 tbsp desiccated coconut
- 200 ml coconut milk
- 2 tbsp curry
- 1 bunch of spring onions

- 2 peaches (ripe)

**preparation**

1. For the peach and fish curry, clean the catfish and cut into pieces. Season with soy sauce, lime juice, salt and pepper.
2. Peel and grate some ginger. Peel and finely chop the clove of garlic. Core and finely chop the chilli pepper.
3. Put all ingredients except for the spring onions and the peaches in a solid cooking container and cook (at 100 °C for 10 minutes).
4. Clean the spring onions and cut into fine rings, peel the peaches and cut into pieces. Add to the remaining ingredients and cook everything together (at 100 °C for 5 minutes).

## 81. Fish cabbage roulade

**ingredients**

- 400 g fish fillets (salmon, char, trout, pike)
- 600 ml cream (liquid)
- 4 yolks
- Pepper (freshly ground)
- salt
- 10 ml lemon juice
- 1 pinch of cayenne pepper
- 8 pcs. Herb leaves (or cabbage leaves)

**preparation**

1. Mince fillets and freeze briefly, mix with cream and yolk in a moulinette to a smooth

mass, season with salt, pepper and a dash of lemon juice.
2. Remove the stalk from the cabbage leaves and boil them individually in salted water, drain well, spread the filling on top and roll up.
3. Layer with the final side in an ovenproof dish and cook in a preheated oven for about 30 minutes.
4. Pour cream / cream mixture over them if necessary.

## 82. Salmon trout pie from the steamer

**ingredients**

- 1 onion (small)
- 2 tbsp butter
- 750 g salmon trout fillet
- 90 g white bread
- 1 pc egg
- salt
- pepper
- nutmeg
- 350 ml cream
- 1 tbsp dill (chopped)
- Butter (for greasing) **preparation**

1. For the salmon trout pie, cut the onion into fine cubes and place in a solid cooking container with the butter. Cover with aluminum foil and steam (at 100 °C for 4 minutes).
2. Rinse the trout fillets, pat dry and remove the skin. Chill one fillet, cut the rest into cubes and add to the onions.
3. Debark the white bread, cut into cubes, place in the cooking container along with the egg, salt, pepper and nutmeg.
4. Add cream and mix all ingredients.
5. Cover and let steep in the refrigerator for 1 hour. Then puree. The mass must not get warm. Add the dill and mix in.
6. Pour half of the mixture into a greased oblong dish, smooth it out and place the trout fillet on top. Spread the rest of the mixture on top, smooth it out and cover. Place the dish on the wire rack in the steamer (at 90 °C for 60-70 minutes).

## 83. Fish patties with garden herbs

**ingredients**

- 500 g fish fillets (white ones such as pikeperch, plaice)
- 1 pc onion
- 2 bunch of garden herbs (e.g. basil, thyme, oregano, chives)
- 1 teaspoon mustard (coarse)
- 2 pc eggs
- 1 piece of lemon (untreated, juice and zest of it)
- 5 tbsp breadcrumbs
- Salt pepper
- Olive oil (for frying)

**preparation**

1. For the fish patties with garden herbs, if necessary, first free the fish fillets from the bones with tweezers and cut into small cubes.
2. Peel the onion and cut into small cubes. Cut the herbs into fine strips. Mix with the remaining ingredients and season with salt and pepper.
3. Shape patties with damp hands and fry on both sides in a hot pan in a little olive oil.
4. The Fischlaibchen with garden herbs in a preheated oven at 180 degrees about 20 minutes to finish cooking and serve immediately.

## 84. Greek fish soup (Kakavia)

**ingredients**

- 1.5kg Mediterranean fish (gurnard, red mullet, scorpionfish, or 600 g fish fi)
- 1.5l fish stock (or water)
- 4 shallots
- 3 tomatoes
- 2 carrots
- 3 potatoes (small)
- 2 cloves of garlic
- 1 bay leaf
- 1 sprig (s) of dill
- 1 sprig (s) of parsley
- some leaf celery
- 3 tbsp lemon juice

- 4 tbsp olive oil
- Sea salt (from the mill) **preparation**

1. Cut the shallots into rings and sweat in olive oil until translucent. Cut the carrots and potatoes into cubes and add to the onions with the chopped garlic. Pour fish stock or water on top. Add the bay leaf and simmer for about 15 minutes. Meanwhile, scale, wash, fillet and debone the fish. Cut the fillets into bite-sized pieces, season with salt and place in the stock. Let it steep for 5-10 minutes over low heat. In the meantime, blanch (scald) the tomatoes, peel and core, cut into cubes and add to the soup. Season to taste with lemon juice and sea salt. Garnish with the plucked parsley, dill and the chopped celery leaves.

## 85. Salmon with Fennel and Orange from the Air Fryer

**Ingredients**

- 3 Tablespoons olive oil
- 1 orange
- 300g salmon
- 1 fennel
- 1 Bunch dill
- Salt pepper **Preparation**

1. Cut the orange and fennel into even slices and season with a dash of olive oil and some salt and pepper. Bake at 160 ° C for 10 minutes.
2. Now put the bunch dill on the fennel and the oranges and embed the salmon on it.

Season again with a little salt, pepper, and olive oil and grate some orange peel on the fish. Bake again for 10 minutes at 160 ° C in the Airfryer and ready!

## 86. Lemon Crust Salmon

**ingredients**

- 250 g pollack fillet
- 1 piece of lemon (approx. 60 g)
- 1 pinch of iodine salt
- 1 1/2 tsp wheat flour (whole grain)
- 2 teaspoons of sunflower oil
- 1 pinch of black pepper

**preparation**

1. Place the defrosted salmon on a plate and drizzle with lemon on both sides.
2. Then salt and pepper on both sides and cover with a little flour.
3. Heat the oil in a pan, then fry the salmon on both sides.

4. Depending on the pieces' thickness and whether the salmon was already completely thawed, the fish is cooked after 10 minutes.

## 87. Orange salmon with nut rice

**ingredients**

- 250 g basmati whole grain rice
- salt
- 1 organic orange
- 40 g herbs (1 handful; parsley and dill)
- tbsp olive oil
- pepper
- 600 g salmon fillet (4 salmon fillets)
- 50 g salted cashew nuts

**Preparation steps**

1. Cook rice in salted water until bite-proof according to the package instructions.
2. In the meantime, wash the orange off hot, pat dry, rub the peel finely and squeeze out the

juice. Wash herbs, shake dry, chop and mix with orange juice and peel, 4 tablespoons of olive oil, salt, and pepper for the marinade. Brush a baking dish with residual oil. Rinse salmon under cold water, pat dry, and turn in the marinade.

3. Roughly chop the nuts. Spread rice in the form, mix in nuts and put fish fillets on top. Drizzle with the rest of the marinade and cook in the preheated oven at 200 ° C (fan oven 180 ° C; gas: setting 3) for about 20 minutes.

## 88. Cured Salmon with Betabel

**Ingredients**
- 2 cups of grain salt
- 2 tablespoons of yellow lemon zest
- 2 tablespoons of orange zest
- 2 tablespoons fresh dill
- 10 pieces of fat pepper, crushed
- 1/2 cup of brown sugar
- 2 cups of beets cut into slices
- 2 kilos of fresh salmon full fish

**Preparation**
1. A medium bowl mix the grain salt with lemon and orange zest, dill, pepper, and sugar. Reservation.
2. A tray with self-adhering plastic spread the beet blades until covering the

surface, add a bit of the bowl mixture above the beets, add the salmon and cover completely with the remaining mixture of the bowl.
3. Perfectly wraps salmon, so that the entire surface is covered with beets and plastic.
4. Refrigerate the salmon for 1 day so that the flavors are impregnated.
5. Remove from refrigeration, discover the salmon in the wrapper, and remove the salt as much as possible until it is clean.
6. Cut the preparation into thin slices, serve and enjoy.

## 89. Moroccan fish skewers

**ingredients**

- ½ tsp coriander seeds
- 1 tsp cumin
- 5 black peppercorns
- 2 dried chili peppers
- saffron threads (1 packet)
- onion
- garlic cloves
- 1 fresh coriander
- 1 lime
- 1 tbsp red wine vinegar
- tbsp olive oil
- sea-salt
- 400 g loach fillet
- 200 g swordfish fillet

**Preparation steps**

1. Roast the coriander seeds, cumin and peppercorns in a pan until an aromatic smoke rises.

2. Grind the dried chili peppers and saffron threads in a mortar or lightning chopper.
3. Peel onion and garlic and chop finely. Wash coriander, shake dry. Pluck leaves and finely chop.
4. Squeeze the lime. Mix the ground spices, onions, garlic and coriander in a bowl with 3 tablespoons of lime juice, vinegar and olive oil to form a seasoning mixture (chermoula) and season salt.
5. Rinse the fish fillets, pat dry and cut each into approx. 2 cm cubes. Turn the fish in about 2/3 of the chermoula and leave to marinate in the refrigerator for at least 1-2 hours.
6. Place the fish pieces on 4 long wooden skewers and grill them over medium-hot charcoal or in a grill pan for 2 minutes on each side. Serve with the rest of the chermoula.

## 90. Stuffed salmon roll from the grill

**ingredients**
- 600 g salmon fillet
- Sea salt
- 100 g ham (air-dried) ☐ 150 g sheep's cheese
- Pepper (fresh from the mill) **preparation**

1. For the filled salmon roll from the grill, let the NORDSEE sales team cut fresh, practically boneless salmon fillet into approx. 1 cm thick and 15 cm long slices (similar to beef rolls).
2. Place 1-2 slices of air-dried ham on each slice of salmon and spread the cream cheese on top.

3. Roll up the salmon fillets and fix them with a toothpick or tie them with cotton thread.
4. Season the outside of the salmon rolls with a little sea salt and freshly ground pepper.
5. Grill the filled salmon rolls on aluminum foil for about 18 minutes at not too high a heat. Carefully turn the filled salmon roll from the grill a few times.

## 91. Tuna on a stick

**ingredients**

- 4 pieces of tuna (approx. 120 g each)
- 100 g of grammes
- salt
- Pepper (from the mill)
- 4 tbsp sesame oil
- 2 tbsp sesame seeds (toasted)
- 50 g parsley (chopped)
- 100 g spring onions (finely chopped)
- 4 wooden skewers (watered)

**preparation**

1. For the tuna on a stick, first salt the tuna, place on a watered wooden skewer and brush all over with sesame oil.

2. Chop the grams and toast them in a pan. Add the spring onions and roast briefly. Mix in the pepper, toasted sesame seeds and parsley.
3. Clean the preheated grill.
4. Quickly grill the tuna on the stick all around on each side, place briefly on the warming rack, sprinkle with the goblet mixture and let it steep briefly.
5. Drizzle the tuna on a stick with a little sesame oil and serve.
6. GRILL METHOD: hot all around, but only briefly
7. GRILL TIME: approx. 2 minutes at approx. 200 ° C, then let rest briefly

## 92. grilled sardines

**ingredients**
- 1 kg of small sardines (or anchovies)
- Flour
- Lemon wedges for garnish ☐ For the marinade:
- 1/2 bunch of parsley
- 2 cloves of garlic
- 4 tbsp olive oil
- Juice of half a lemon
- salt
- Pepper (freshly ground) **preparation**

1. Cut open the sardines on the belly and remove the innards. Rinse with cold water and pat dry carefully.
2. For the marinade, pluck the parsley leaves from the stalks, peel and finely chop the garlic cloves. Mix all ingredients in a large bowl. Put the fish in and leave to marinate for about 1 hour.
3. Remove the sardines from the marinade and dust them lightly with flour. Grill on the grill for about 3 minutes on each side. The grilled sardines with lemon slices and fresh white bread dish.

## 93. Grilled Sea bream

**ingredients**

- 4 pieces of sea bream
- 2 pieces of lemon
- 3 tbsp thyme
- 4 tbsp sea salt
- 200 ml of olive oil
- 4 tbsp lemon pepper
- BBQ seasoning **preparation**

1. Mix the ingredients into a marinade for the grilled sea bream and marinate the sea bream for at least 30 minutes. Then place the fish on the grill and season with a BBQ spice while grilling.

2. Grill the fish until the skin is crispy. The grilled sea bream dish and serve.

## 94. Grilled prawns

**ingredients**

- 16 prawns (without shell)
- 2 courgettes (medium)
- 4 tbsp oil
- 1 teaspoon salt
- 1 teaspoon lemon (juice) **preparation**

1. Place the crab tails with the sliced zucchinis alternately on 4 oiled wooden skewers. Drizzle with oil and sprinkle with salt. Grill under the heated grillage for 5 to 8 minutes, drizzle with the juice of a lemon.
2. Bring to the table with white wine and white bread.

3. 20 min.
4. Tip: Zucchini are a type of pumpkin and are therefore low in calories, rich in vitamins and easy to digest - just the thing for a light diet!

## 95. Grilled scampi on wok vegetables

**ingredients**

*For the scampi:*

- 500 g scampi (red)
- 1 tbsp peanut oil
- 2 tbsp garlic
- 2 tsp ginger (freshly chopped)
- 4 spring onions
- 100 g paprika (red and green) *For the sauce:*
- 200 ml chicken breasts
- 2 tbsp Shaoxing rice wine (or white wine)
- 3 tbsp soy sauce
- 2 tbsp Paradeismark

- 1 tbsp cornstarch **preparation**
1. Heat the wok vigorously and then add the peanut oil. Fry the garlic and ginger in it. Add the chopped peppers and spring onions. Roast all the ingredients again. Pour the previously mixed sauce over the vegetables. Halve the prawns and remove the intestines. Season with salt and pepper and fry with the meat side up. Finally, arrange the vegetables and place the fried prawns on top.

## 96. Grilled seafood skewers

**ingredients** *For the skewers*

- 1 zucchini
- 200 g salmon fillet ready to cook, skinless
- 200 g pikeperch fillet ready to cook, with skin
- 200 g shrimp ready to cook, peeled and deveined
- 2 untreated limes
- 1 tsp red peppercorns
- ½ tsp black peppercorns
- sea-salt
- 4 tbsp olive oil
- For the dip

- 500 g
- natural yoghurt
- pepper from the mill
- sugar

**Preparation steps**

2. Wash and clean the zucchini and cut into 1 cm thick slices. Wash the fish, pat dry and cut into bite-sized cubes. Wash the prawns. Rinse the limes with hot water, rub the peel of one lime and squeeze out the juice. Cut the remaining lime into slices. Coarsely crush the peppercorns in a mortar and mix with a generous pinch of salt, the oil and half of the lime juice. Place the fish cubes alternately with the zucchini slices and the prawns on kebab skewers and coat with the lime marinade. Let it steep for 30 minutes.

3. For the dip, mix the yoghurt with the rest of the lime juice, mix with salt, pepper and a pinch of sugar, fill into bowls and garnish with the lime zest. Place the skewers together with the lime slices on a hot grill and grill for 8-10 minutes, turning them occasionally. Serve with the dip.

4.

## 97. Fish skewer with tarator sauce

**ingredients**
- 700 g firm fish fillet (sword or tuna)
- 1 lemon (juice)
- olive oil
- Paprika powder (noble sweet)
- Sea salt (from the mill)
- Pepper (from the mill)
- Bay leaves (fresh) *For the sauce:*
- 100 g walnuts (peeled)
- 3 cloves of garlic
- 2 slice (s) of white bread (without rind)
- 150 ml of olive oil
- 1 lemon (juice)
- Sea salt (from the mill)

- Pepper (from the mill) **preparation**

1. Cut the fish fillet into approx. 2 cm thick cubes and marinate with lemon juice, olive oil, paprika powder, sea salt and pepper for approx. 1 hour. Then stick the fish pieces alternately with a bay leaf each on a large or several small metal skewers. Grill over charcoal if possible, otherwise fry in a Teflon pan. Mix all the ingredients in a mixer to make a homogeneous sauce for the sauce. Arrange the fried skewers, serve the sauce separately.

## 98. Grilled alpine salmon

**ingredients**

- Alpine salmon
- olive oil
- Spices (of your choice)
- Herbs (of your choice)

**preparation**

1. For the alpine salmon, wash the ready-tocook fish well and pat dry.
2. Brush the fish with olive oil and rub the inside and outside with your choice of spices. Put herbs of your choice in the belly of the fish.
3. Place the fish on the Grill and grill for about 7 minutes.

## 99. Mediterranean feta in foil

**ingredients**
- 1 clove (s) of garlic
- 2 tbsp Rama Culinesse plant cream
- 1 pc shallot
- 1 tbsp pine nuts
- 6 sprigs of thyme (alternatively 1 teaspoon of dried thyme)
- 5 pcs. Olives (without stone)
- 1 teaspoon capers
- 4 pieces of anchovy fillets
- 20 g tomatoes (sun-dried)
- 6 cherry tomatoes
- 2 pieces of feta (150g each)

**preparation**
1. Peel and finely dice shallot and garlic. Roast the pine nuts in a pan without fat, over medium heat until golden brown. Roughly chop the thyme, olives, capers, anchovies, pine nuts and sun-dried tomatoes and mix with the shallots, garlic and vegetable cream.
2. Wash and slice cherry tomatoes. Spread out two pieces of aluminium foil and place one feta on each, spread the tomato slices and rama vegetable cream on top. Fold the aluminium foil into parcels and place on the grill for about 15 minutes.

## 100. Ling fish in the foil

**ingredients**

- 300 g mushrooms
- 3 carrots
- 125 ml classic vegetable broth
- salt
- pepper
- 600 g ling fish fillet (4 ling fish fillets)
- 2 poles
- lemongrass

**Preparation steps**

1. Clean the mushrooms and cut them in slices.
2. Clean, peel and wash the carrots. First cut lengthways into thin slices, then into fine strips.

3. Put the carrot strips in a saucepan with 5 tablespoons of stock, add the mushroom slices and cook covered for about 5 minutes over medium heat. Season with salt and pepper.
4. Layout 4 large pieces of aluminium foil (approx. 30x30 cm each) on the work surface. Fold up the edges a little so that nothing can leak out later.
5. Divide the vegetables into 4 pieces of aluminium foil. Rinse the fish fillets, pat dry and place on the vegetables. Salt and pepper.
6. Clean and wash lemongrass, peel off the hard outer leaves; Finely chop the soft inside and sprinkle over the fish fillets.
7. Drizzle 2 tablespoons of vegetable stock over 1 serving. Fold the aluminium foil tightly into parcels and grill on the hot grill for 1215 minutes.

# CONCLUSION

Keep in mind that seafood is not only delicious, but it can also be beneficial to your health.

www.ingramcontent.com/pod-product-compliance
Lightning Source LLC
Chambersburg PA
CBHW050027130526
44590CB00042B/2015